WORLD CUP
2018 RUSSIA
ESSENTIAL
GUIDE

The Complete Book of
Everything World Cup Soccer 2018

ULTIMATE WORLD CUP BOOKS

DUTTON

DUTTON

An imprint of Penguin Random House LLC
375 Hudson Street
New York, New York 10014

ISBN 9780525539445 (trade paperback)
ISBN 9780525539452 (eBook)

Printed in the United States of America

1   3   5   7   9   10   8   6   4   2

Set in Arial
Designed by Paula Sadler

This publication is designed to provide accurate and authoritative
information in regard to the subject matter covered. It is sold with the
understanding that the publisher is not engaged in rendering legal,
accounting, or other professional services. If you require legal advice or
other expert assistance, you should seek the services
of a competent professional.

FIFA.com rankings accurate as of May 7, 2018.

WELCOME TO WORLD CUP 2018

After over three years of qualification matches, the FIFA World Cup will open in Russia on June 14, 2018.

Thirty-two nations from six confederations around the world will make a bid for the most cherished cup in world soccer. The teams have been drawn into eight groups (A–H), with four teams each. They'll face every opponent in their group, and the top two teams will advance to the knockout rounds.

Many players will have competed into the early summer with their club teams in domestic leagues around the world. But playing for your country is a different kind of honor—and another challenge—altogether. They'll need to quickly settle into their first games if they want to move past the groups.

There are some notable absences in 2018—Chile, Italy, the Netherlands, and the United States all failed to qualify—and some intriguing newcomers as well. Will we see a new champion this year?

GROUP A

EGYPT • RUSSIA • SAUDI ARABIA • URUGUAY

JUNE 14
Russia vs. Saudi Arabia

JUNE 15
Egypt vs. Uruguay

JUNE 19
Russia vs. Egypt

JUNE 20
Uruguay vs. Saudi Arabia

JUNE 25
Saudi Arabia vs. Egypt
Uruguay vs. Russia

Group A looks to be one of the easiest in the Cup, and that should come as a big relief to the Russians. They'll desperately want to win their first game, both for fan morale and to have any hopes of moving through to the next round. Standing in their way? Clear group favorite Uruguay, an exciting Egyptian squad, and an ambitious Saudi Arabian side.

EGYPT

COACH: HÉCTOR CÚPER
TEAM NICKNAME: THE PHARAOHS
PREVIOUS APPEARANCES: 2 • **WINS:** 0 • **FIFA RANKING:** 31

Egypt is back in the World Cup after a 28-year absence. The team's record in decades past has been a disappointment to their fans—and they have yet to ever win a World Cup match—but as last year's runner-up at the prestigious Africa Cup of Nations, the Egyptians have reason to feel optimistic.

Egypt's defense had an excellent record in qualifying matches. By using many players to lie deep and guard the goal, they limited most of their opponents to no more than one goal per game. Such a defensive style of play is not always fun to watch. But it gets results and will likely come in handy against teams like Russia and Saudi Arabia, which might not have much attacking power, and teams like Uruguay—whose big-name offensive players will still find the Egyptian defense tough to break down. Behind the defense, Egypt's goalkeeper and captain, Essam El-Hadary (age 45), is set to become the oldest player in World Cup history.

But for Egyptians, this Cup will center on one man: right winger Mohamed "Mo" Salah. The star Liverpool player and 2018 PFA Player of the Year has been instrumental to his club team's fast-paced style this past season. His two goals against Congo in qualifying earned Egypt its spot at the World Cup. Look for Mo Salah and midfielder Mohamed Elneny to create chances on their side of the pitch.

RUSSIA

COACH: STANISLAV CHERCHESOV
TEAM NICKNAME: SBORNAYA ("NATIONAL TEAM")
PREVIOUS APPEARANCES: 10 • **WINS:** 0 • **FIFA RANKING:** 65

Russia automatically qualified by hosting the tournament, but they now have an uphill battle ahead of them. Several key issues could make or break Russia's performance. Their squad consists mostly of players from the Russian leagues; teammates are familiar with one another's styles, but Russia lacks the star power of many of the other Cup teams. Their best-known player, Igor Denisov, could have provided creativity and technical ability in midfield—but after conflicts with the team coach, it looks like he's off the squad.

Russia's aging defense could also be a cause of concern, especially since their preferred team setup creates a lot of work for them.

Veteran defenders like Yuri Zhirkov and Dmitri Kombarov must keep up with the rigorous demands of their group matches, but youngsters like Viktor Vasin, Fedor Kudryashov, and Georgi Dzhikiya could help out their older counterparts. The Russian goalkeeper and captain, Igor Akinfeev, should provide a steady hand behind them, and their main forward player, striker Fedor Smolov, has been a top goal scorer for his club team, FC Krasnodar.

The pressures of hosting can become a huge burden to the home side (ask Brazil!), but they can also galvanize players to unexpected heights. Will Team Russia crack under the pressure, or will they find hometown glory?

SAUDI ARABIA

COACH: JUAN ANTONIO PIZZI
TEAM NICKNAME: THE GREEN FALCONS
PREVIOUS APPEARANCES: 4 • WINS: 0 • FIFA RANKING: 63

It's the Saudis' first appearance at the World Cup since 2006. And this time around, they're managed by the former Chile national team coach Juan Antonio Pizzi. (He helped his former side win the 2015 Copa América.) The Saudi squad will all know one another like brothers, because most have played for years with the same top teams of the Saudi Arabian club league.

Forward Mohammad Al-Sahlawi will give Saudi Arabia its best chance at goals: He tied for the leading goal scorer in World Cup qualification with 16 goals. He'll be supported by midfielders Taisir Al-Jassim and Nawaf Al-Abed. Coach Pizzi has also been experimenting with adding more attacking excitement to his teams. That means potentially giving untested young players from the Saudi league a real shot at getting coveted game time.

Despite being among the lowest-ranked teams in the tournament, Saudi Arabia did beat another 2018 World Cup team, Japan, to qualify. They could prove very dangerous to a few countries in the tournament, especially fellow Group A team Russia. Could Saudi Arabia open the World Cup with a home upset?

URUGUAY

COACH: ÓSCAR TABÁREZ
TEAM NICKNAME: LA CELESTE ("THE SKY BLUE")
PREVIOUS APPEARANCES: 12 • WINS: 2 • FIFA RANKING: 21

The clear favorites of the group, Uruguay should feel delighted with its relatively lucky draw. During World Cup qualifying, it placed second in its challenging South American group. But the team does have some vulnerabilities: They've struggled in more recent tournaments, crashing out early in the last two Copa Américas. An opponent able to quickly counterattack could cause Uruguay problems as their defense tries to settle into the tournament.

Scoring shouldn't be much of a problem for Uruguay in the group stages, especially with world-renowned attacking threats like Barcelona's Luis Suárez and Paris Saint-Germain's Edinson Cavani. The pair have scored over 92 goals for their country! When they're on their game, Suárez and Cavani are the kind of players who can create miracle chances and completely turn a game on its head. They'll be joined by talented youngsters like Matías Vecino, Rodrigo Bentancur, and Nahitan Nández.

The keys to Uruguay's success will be quickly getting the ball out from the back to these attacking players ... and making sure that Suárez, whose penchant for bizarre World Cup controversies has earned him match bans in the past, will put team and country first.

GROUP B

IRAN • MOROCCO • PORTUGAL • SPAIN

JUNE 15
Morocco vs. Iran
Portugal vs. Spain

JUNE 20
Portugal vs. Morocco
Iran vs. Spain

JUNE 25
Spain vs. Morocco
Iran vs. Portugal

At first glance, Group B looks predictable. European powerhouses Spain and Portugal boast world-famous rosters; Iran and Morocco simply don't come close to matching them. But Spain and Portugal may be in for a surprise or two. Iran and Morocco are still technically gifted sides whose defenses will make life very tough for the Iberian neighbors.

IRAN

COACH: CARLOS QUEIROZ
TEAM NICKNAME: TEAM MELLI
PREVIOUS APPEARANCES: 4 • WINS: 0 • FIFA RANKING: 32

Iran may not score many goals, or come out on top in many of their World Cup games—their last Cup win was a 2–1 victory over the United States 20 years ago—but good luck scoring against them in 2018! Team Melli are unbeaten in their most recent friendly matches, went undefeated in their qualifying games, and conceded only three goals in the first stage of their campaign.

Experienced and practical Portuguese manager Carlos Queiroz has set his team up with a defensive style of play that will be unbelievably difficult for any competition to break down. Iran will hope to frustrate opponents, win the ball back, and then immediately counterattack. They must move the ball forward as quickly as possible and try to make up for their relative lack of passing ability with direct long balls up to their forwards.

Iran's brightest hope for goals will come from 22-year-old striker Sardar Azmoun, who plays club soccer in Russia. He's been likened by his countrymen to Lionel Messi and scouted by major European clubs, and he has the best goals-to-game ratio of any Iranian player. Azmoun lives for big games and loves playing for the national team. Will this be his summer?

MOROCCO

COACH: HERVÉ RENARD
TEAM NICKNAME: ATLAS LIONS
PREVIOUS APPEARANCES: 4 • WINS: 0 • FIFA RANKING: 40

Morocco became the first African side to get out of a World Cup group stage 32 years ago, but it hasn't been back to the tournament since France 1998. Now it's a well-balanced, hardworking team with a steely defense. The Moroccans placed at the top of their qualifying group and did not concede a single goal in their campaign. They'll hope to continue that record, even against the likes of Spain and Portugal.

Their defense is led by their captain, and perhaps best-known player, Medhi Benatia. He'll be making heroic tackles and knocking opponents off the ball to regain possession. Benatia's veteran experience with the Morocco national team and reassuring presence will be invaluable to younger players like Hakim Ziyech and Nordin Amrabat. These two midfielders will look to move the ball up the pitch and hopefully score some goals while still providing defensive cover. Forward Ayoub El Kaabi must also provide clinical goal finishing if Morocco is to have any hopes of leading Group B.

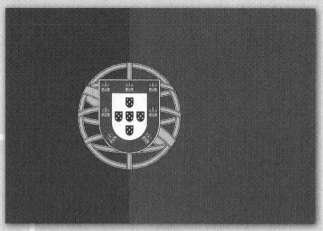

PORTUGAL

COACH: FERNANDO SANTOS
TEAM NICKNAME: SELEÇÃO DAS QUINAS ("TEAM OF FIVE")
PREVIOUS APPEARANCES: 6 • WINS: 0 • FIFA RANKING: 3

Portugal was the surprise winner of Euro 2016, and while its odds of winning this World Cup may not be as high as other teams', it still hopes to go far in the tournament. First, they'll need to settle on their defense. Central defender and vice-captain Pepe is nearing the end of his career, and while he'll need a faster-paced, levelheaded partner, Portugal has yet to find a consistent pairing.

Going forward, Portugal's options will be the envy (and dread) of many teams at the tournament. Cristiano Ronaldo will be the center of the team's, and its opponents', attention—not just for his scoring prowess (81 goals in total for his country) and his success at club Real Madrid, but also because he wouldn't have it any other way. He and Argentine rival Lionel Messi are considered the greatest soccer players alive today, and Ronaldo in particular is known for his hotheaded drive, competitive spirit, and ability to feed off fan energy (positive or otherwise).

Having such a talismanic figure in your squad can be a blessing and a curse. If Portugal relies too heavily on one legendary player, then its opponents will know exactly where to focus their efforts. Portugal's success may well depend on whether they can find a balance between tapping into their hero's immense talents and keeping other forward options open.

SPAIN

COACH: JULEN LOPETEGUI
TEAM NICKNAME: LA ROJA ("THE RED")
PREVIOUS APPEARANCES: 14 • WINS: 0 • FIFA RANKING: 6

Spain has an odd recent World Cup history. They won the Cup in 2010, only to crash out of the group stages in 2014. Now, they're back among the favorites to lift the trophy in 2018. They should feel confident: Their roster is a who's who of some the world's greatest players at top clubs around Europe.

Goalkeeper David de Gea, the best in the world, stops shots and saves games for club Manchester United with his stunning reflexes. Central defenders like Sergio Ramos and Gerard Piqué can close down any offense and don't shy away from physical challenges on the ball. Out on the sides, hardworking and crafty fullbacks Daniel Carvajal and Jordi Alba provide defensive support while readily joining in dynamic attacking play. Legendary midfielders Sergio Busquets, Andrés Iniesta, Nacho Monreal, Isco, and Thiago Alcantara dominate games, and forwards David Silva and Diego Costa regularly terrify other teams.

Spain's bench has unparalleled depth: Players who would be stars on other teams in the tournament will struggle just to make Spain's starting squad. With such a multitude of options, particularly in midfield, they can adjust their play and adeptly deal with injuries as needed. But can they make it all the way to the final?

GROUP C

AUSTRALIA • DENMARK • FRANCE • PERU

JUNE 16
France vs. Australia
Peru vs. Denmark

JUNE 21
Denmark vs. Australia
France vs. Peru

JUNE 26
Australia vs. Peru
Denmark vs. France

France is the clear favorite to top the group, but Australia, Denmark, and Peru could prove to be tricky opponents. All teams are poised to bring attacking intensity, confident ball playing, and hordes of passionate fans to the competition.

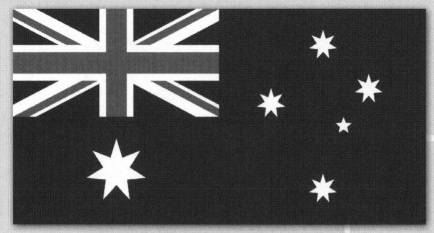

AUSTRALIA

COACH: BERT VAN MARWIJK

TEAM NICKNAME: THE SOCCEROOS

PREVIOUS APPEARANCES: 4 • WINS: 0 • FIFA RANKING: 39

Australia's road to the World Cup hasn't been easy. Their qualifying campaign included tens of thousands of miles covered across their Asian division, and it took two extra playoff rounds for them just to make it into Group C. Then managerial controversies left the team coachless just a few months before the start of the tournament—and on the world stage, that kind of drama is the very last thing a team needs.

The players, now guided by emergency replacement coach Bert van Marwijk, must use every asset they have to compete in this group. Socceroo star Tim Cahill, Australia's famous forward, is surely at the end of his career—at age 38, he'll probably be the oldest forward in the tournament—but he's still their go-to for goals. Youngsters like Aaron Mooy must also bring new energy to forward play and provide another attacking outlet. Australia will need their attacking players to hit their stride early, as they've been weak defensively and struggled to shut down their opponents. If you can't contain them, outscore them!

DENMARK

COACH: ÅGE HAREIDE

TEAM NICKNAME: DANISH DYNAMITE

PREVIOUS APPEARANCES: 4 • WINS: 0 • FIFA RANKING: 12

Denmark could easily be described as a "dark horse" team, largely thanks to the creative skill of talismanic midfielder Christian Eriksen. In addition to quickly moving the ball forward and helping dictate the tempo of play, Eriksen will definitely get in on the goal scoring as well. He scored 11 goals in 12 qualifying matches, and led Denmark to comfortable, sweeping victories against teams like Poland and the Republic of Ireland.

The second-highest qualification scorer? Midfielder Thomas Delaney. He'll play to the left of Eriksen and create another attacking threat. Delaney has said he won't settle for less than the knockout rounds: "I don't just want to play three games and then have to pack my bags and go home...We're a small country, but expectations are obviously high."

Up ahead of the midfield, a forward player like Nicolai Jørgensen or Nicklas Bendtner will play as a lone striker, looking to receive the ball at the far end of the pitch while constantly pestering the opposition's back line. With so many dangerous players in Denmark's ranks, Delaney may well get his wish.

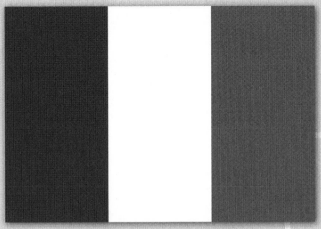

FRANCE

COACH: DIDIER DESCHAMPS
TEAM NICKNAME: LES BLEUS ("THE BLUES")
PREVIOUS APPEARANCES: 14 • WINS: 1 • FIFA RANKING: 9

Among the favorites to win the World Cup, this team of all-stars will benefit from particularly exciting options going forward. The center of their attack will likely be Antoine Griezmann, the Atlético Madrid striker with a keen nose for gold. But be sure to watch out for Olivier Giroud, France's top goal scorer, and fast-paced forwards Kylian Mbappé and Ousmane Dembélé.

The midfield is also packed with talent, like N'Golo Kanté and superstar Paul Pogba, a box-to-box midfielder (as in, willing and able to cover all ground from one end of the pitch to the other). On paper, it's hard to see who could stop these players, all world renowned for jaw-dropping skill, attacking flair, and the ability to single-handedly change the course of a game.

But for all the incredible names on its roster, France sometimes struggles to bring together their individual talents as a cohesive unit. They lost Euro 2016 to Portugal on home soil and have had an uneven qualification campaign. Tactics matter. Bold, brilliant, and fiercely competitive players can win a country trophies, but only if they fit together as a team. Will France find a way to play its forwards and midfielders together in a way that gets the best out of these immense players? Or will France actually suffer from too many good options?

PERU

COACH: RICARDO GARECA
TEAM NICKNAME: LA BLANQUIRROJA ("THE WHITE AND RED")
PREVIOUS APPEARANCES: 4 • WINS: 0 • FIFA RANKING: 11

Welcome back, Peru! It's been 36 long years since the South American side qualified for the tournament, and this bright, hardworking squad is determined to make the moment count.

One of the keys to Peru's success has been the seamless blending of older players with up-and-coming youth. The team will be led by veteran goalkeeper Pedro Gallese and sturdy defenders like captain Alberto Rodríguez. Their years of experience and consistency will allow the younger players to confidently attack. Up top, a pairing of older forwards Jefferson Farfán and Paolo Guerrero and younger midfielder Christian Cueva could make for a deadly combination of great player positioning and pacey runs forward.

The center of Peru's team will hopefully be Guerrero. The top-level forward is possibly facing a ban from the Cup because of off-pitch controversies, and Peruvians everywhere will be anxiously waiting to find out if he'll play in Russia. With 32 goals total, he's Peru's all-time top goal scorer.

GROUP D

ARGENTINA • CROATIA • ICELAND • NIGERIA

JUNE 16
Argentina vs. Iceland
Croatia vs. Nigeria

JUNE 21
Argentina vs. Croatia

JUNE 22
Nigeria vs. Iceland

JUNE 26
Iceland vs. Croatia
Nigeria vs. Argentina

Argentina may be the front-runner of this group, but it's in for a rocky road to the knockout rounds. As in Group C, the lesser-known teams of Group D are full of exciting talent. If Argentina wants to win the group, it'll need to go toe to toe with Croatia's technical ability, find a way through Iceland's fortresslike defense, and contain the menacing threat of Nigeria's lightning-fast counterattacks.

ARGENTINA

COACH: JORGE SAMPAOLI
TEAM NICKNAME: LA ALBICELESTE ("THE WHITE AND SKY BLUE")
PREVIOUS APPEARANCES: 16 • **WINS:** 2 • **FIFA RANKING:** 4

Argentina has a wealth of talent on its roster, but for the team, this summer was always going to be about Lionel Messi. Messi is considered by many to be the best player alive, and arguably one of the greatest of all time. This will likely be the legend's last chance at a World Cup. His legions of fans have been waiting to see him in this Cup for years—but it almost didn't happen.

After the agony of narrowly losing the 2014 World Cup to Germany, and the heartbreak of losing Copa América 2015 and Copa América Centenario (2016) to Chile, Messi quit the national team. Unsurprisingly, Argentina struggled without him. Thankfully, he soon rejoined the squad, and it was ultimately his hat trick in their last qualifying match that got them through to the final tournament. Messi doesn't need to win a World Cup to be one of the greats—but he'll want it more than ever.

Supporting his dream will be outstanding senior players Sergio Romero, Gonzalo Higuaín, Ángel Di María, Sergio Agüero, Lucas Biglia, and Éver Banega—all likely also facing their last chance at a World Cup trophy. Despite such an impressive roster, it really does come down to Messi, who time after time has carried his team to Cup finals. But it's dangerous to rely too heavily on one man, even one as legendary as Messi. Will this be his year?

CROATIA

COACH: ZLATKO DALIĆ
TEAM NICKNAME: VATRENI ("THE BLAZERS")
PREVIOUS APPEARANCES: 4 • WINS: 0 • FIFA RANKING: 17

Croatia's late switch to manager Zlatko Dalić risks the kind of organizational chaos that you don't want just before a major tournament, but the level of technical ability on display in the Croatian national team will hopefully see them past this challenge. Dalić himself has said, "I have to give all the credit to the players. There wasn't much time for training and preparation...and they stepped up at the most important moment."

Soccer superstar Luka Modrić debuted for the Croatian senior national team in 2006 and has been with them for every major tournament since. Today he's one of the best midfielders in the game, and he'll help dictate their play from the center of the pitch. Modrić has it all: experience, sensational passing ability, and excellent ball control. His creativity in the midfield will give goal scorers like Andrej Kramarić and Mario Mandžukić plenty of opportunities to smash the ball into the net.

In fact, Croatia's midfield is packed with technically gifted, quick-thinking, and quick-footed players who would be the envy of any team. Ivan Perišić, captain Ivan Rakitić, and even 20-year-old Nikola Vlašić are sure to be a nightmare for the rest of Group D. But relative to the quality of their roster, Croatia has underperformed recently at major tournaments. Will they separate themselves from the pack in 2018?

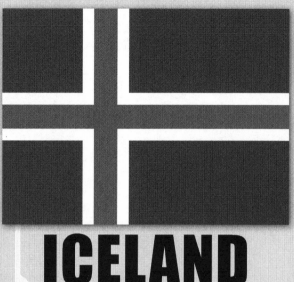

ICELAND

COACH: HEIMIR HALLGRÍMSSON
PREVIOUS APPEARANCES: 0 • WINS: 0 • FIFA RANKING: 22

This is Iceland's first appearance at the World Cup. It's also the smallest nation to ever reach the Cup. But if you think these newcomers will feel overwhelmed by the grandeur of the tournament, think again! Many soccer fans were introduced to Iceland at Euro 2016, the team's first major tournament. They went out in the quarterfinals but not before serving up a humiliating defeat to England and winning the hearts of spectators from around the world.

Forwards Kolbeinn Sigþórsson and Alfreð Finnbogason will be looking for goals, aided by expert midfielder Gylfi Sigurðsson. If Sigurðsson gets his chance (and if he's fully recovered from injury), this set-piece expert will gladly punish opponents' defenses for any mistake they make. Meanwhile, a tough-as-nails Iceland defense will frustrate even the most gifted opposition.

Iceland's population (around 350,000) is smaller than even the city of Moscow's. At Euro 2016, an incredible 10 percent of the nation's population traveled to support their team, and many expect similar numbers to make the pilgrimage to Russia. If their second major tournament is anything like the first, these die-hard fans will be the talk of the World Cup. Look (and listen!) for the Icelandic fans' signature Viking clap as they rally behind their team.

NIGERIA

COACH: GERNOT ROHR
TEAM NICKNAME: THE SUPER EAGLES
PREVIOUS APPEARANCES: 5 • WINS: 0 • FIFA RANKING: 50

Nigeria is historically a very strong African team, and while it's one of the lower-ranked sides in the tournament, this year is no exception. The team is known for both a very sturdy defense and a number of fast players who can quickly win the ball off opponents and charge toward the goal. These counterattacks can take advantage of even the smallest mistakes from the other team, and they could help Nigeria surprise its group rivals—the team came back from behind to beat Argentina 4–2 in a friendly match last year.

Perhaps the most famous member of the current squad, captain John Obi Mikel plays in the midfield for London club Chelsea, where he's won domestic and European championships. Obi Mikel brings years of experience and discipline to the Nigerian team, but he won't have to do all the work: He's joined by fellow Chelsea player Victor Moses and Leicester forward Ahmed Musa, plus exciting young talent like Kelechi Iheanacho (Leicester) and Alex Iwobi (Arsenal), who also have experience winning trophies with their domestic league clubs.

GROUP E

BRAZIL • COSTA RICA • SERBIA • SWITZERLAND

JUNE 17
Costa Rica vs. Serbia
Brazil vs. Switzerland

JUNE 22
Brazil vs. Costa Rica
Serbia vs. Switzerland

JUNE 27
Switzlerland vs. Costa Rica
Serbia vs. Brazil

Brazil is expected to finish at the top of the group without much trouble, but the other three teams will be relying on their sturdy defenses to keep Brazil goals to a minimum. Anything is possible, and the battle for second place should be close!

BRAZIL

COACH: TITE
TEAM NICKNAME: A SELEÇÃO ("THE TEAM")
PREVIOUS APPEARANCES: 20 • WINS: 5 • FIFA RANKING: 2

It has to be mentioned: Things did not go well for Brazil at their last World Cup. Losing 7–1 to Germany in a semifinal on their own soil was a nightmare for the team and a traumatic event for the nation, but this reenergized squad is out to prove that they've put the past behind them. They looked excellent in qualifying, easily finishing first in their tough South American group, with only one loss at the very beginning of the campaign. They were the first team (besides the home side) to qualify for Russia.

Brazil's coach, Tite, has brought out the best in his star-studded squad. Soccer genius Neymar, who struggled with injury earlier in the year, will still undoubtedly be Brazil's main man again at this World Cup. Neymar's dazzling ball control and dribbling abilities can wreak havoc, and they'll add a creative spark that picks apart even the most stubborn defensive lines. Striker Gabriel Jesus will also constantly challenge opponents' back line. This allows Neymar much more freedom to move around the left side of the pitch and will certainly stretch defenders' coverage. Meanwhile, the excellent passers Paulinho and Philippe Coutinho can also threaten defenders down the sides of the pitch, and ambitious fullbacks Dani Alves and Marcelo provide yet more attacking threats. With so many flashy attacking players, will 2018 be the year of Brazil's redemption?

COSTA RICA

COACH: ÓSCAR RAMÍREZ
TEAM NICKNAME: LOS TICOS
PREVIOUS APPEARANCES: 4 • WINS: 0 • FIFA RANKING: 26

Keylor Navas, Costa Rica's goalkeeper, is probably the best-known player for Los Ticos. His time in La Liga with Real Madrid has earned him respect throughout the soccer world, and he's one of the few players on the Costa Rican team with experience in the most elite leagues of Europe. Having a goalkeeper as your most famous player might not seem glamorous, but Costa Rica doesn't need glamor. Their rock-solid defense got this underdog side all the way to the quarterfinals of the last World Cup. They finished first in their 2014 group with England, Italy, and Uruguay. In the knockout rounds, they held the Netherlands to an agonizing penalty shootout before capitulating. That's Los Ticos—a never-give-in, fight-to-the-last team that works as a unit to exhaust and frustrate their opponents.

Their discipline could help them get out of the group stages again, but they'll still face great obstacles to repeat their past success. One way or another, the team that scores most wins, and while Costa Rica can stop even great teams from scoring, they don't find it easy to score themselves. They'll be depending on players like captain and forward Bryan Ruiz and midfielder Celso Borges to make their chances count and advance them to the next round. It's a long shot, but as anyone who's ever watched or played against them knows, never, ever underestimate Los Ticos.

SERBIA

COACH: MLADEN KRSTAJIĆ
TEAM NICKNAME: BELI ORLOVI (THE EAGLES)
PREVIOUS APPEARANCES: 11 • WINS: 0 • FIFA RANKING: 37

Serbian fans must be very encouraged by their team's prospects for the 2018 World Cup. Since becoming an independent nation in 2006 (they used to play as Yugoslavia and Yugoslavia/Serbia and Montenegro), they missed out on the 2010 and 2014 World Cups. But this time, they suffered only one loss in 10 games and scored 20 goals, more than any other team in their qualifying group.

While older Serbian legends Nemanja Vidić and Dejan Stanković have retired, the team still benefits from the experience of some veteran players in defenders Branislav Ivanović and captain Aleksandar Kolarov. At the heart of Serbia's team, midfielder and vice-captain Nemanja Matić will help defenders close down attacks and control the game. Matić is one of the most successful defensive midfielders in the game today; he's won titles with former club Chelsea and currently plays for Manchester United, where he's been described by the team's manager as "a giant, not for his size but for the way he plays."

All these famous players, defenders included, have scored goals for Serbia. Attacking options like Dušan Tadić, plus youngsters Aleksandar Mitrović and Sergej Milinković-Savić, make Serbia an imposing presence in Group E.

SWITZERLAND

COACH: VLADIMIR PETKOVIĆ
TEAM NICKNAME: LA NATI ("THE NATIONAL TEAM")
PREVIOUS APPEARANCES: 10 • WINS: 0 • FIFA RANKING: 8

Unlike some of its European neighbors, Switzerland doesn't have a famous out-and-out goal scorer to rely on for points—but it still has plenty of attacking power. At the center of the pitch, Granit Xhaka is known for dominating the midfield and creating chances for his team. He's especially good at winning the ball off opponents and quickly driving it forward.

Xhaka is surrounded by pacey players like Xherdan Shaqiri and Steven Zuber, who will take Xhaka's created chances and literally run with them. Stephan Lichtsteiner and Ricardo Rodríguez may play for Switzerland's defense, but look for them to get in on the offensive play too. As fullbacks, they'll charge forward to stretch their opponents and create more options out wide.

Switzerland's attack-minded setup got them to the knockout rounds of Euro 2016, where they narrowly lost on penalty shootouts to another World Cup team, Poland. This soccer-crazy nation has yet to go further than the quarterfinals in a major tournament; will their adventurous style of play push Switzerland to new heights, or will they struggle to get out of their tricky group?

GROUP F

GERMANY • KOREA REPUBLIC • MEXICO • SWEDEN

JUNE 17
Germany vs. Mexico

JUNE 18
Sweden vs. Korea Republic

JUNE 23
Korea Republic vs. Mexico
Germany vs. Sweden

JUNE 27
Korea Republic vs. Germany
Mexico vs. Sweden

One thing's for sure—nobody in this group wanted to draw Germany! Group F is expected to be Germany's to win, so the rest of the teams in this quirky group will be in a desperate fight for that precious second-place spot.

GERMANY

COACH: JOACHIM LÖW

TEAM NICKNAME: DIE MANNSCHAFT ("THE TEAM")

PREVIOUS APPEARANCES: 18 • WINS: 4 • FIFA RANKING: 1

Germany is the reigning champion and among the favorites to win this year. Like the other top teams, it has a roster stacked with world-class talent: Goalkeepers Manuel Neuer and Marc-André ter Stegen are used to making great saves; Joshua Kimmich, Mats Hummels, Jérôme Boateng, and Jonas Hector all work well together in defense; Toni Kroos controls the midfield; Thomas Müller and Mesut Özil relish their roles as playmakers; and, most exciting, newcomer Timo Werner will likely shine as their striker.

Germany has more than talent though: It has a winning tournament mentality. They're good at pacing themselves in the group stages and then ramping up momentum in the later rounds. They're excellent at penalty shootouts—sure to come in handy as the knockout rounds progress. And they're consistent: The last time they didn't make it to at least the semifinals was 1998!

Now, with a World Cup title to their names, many of the players in this lineup will know exactly what it takes to lift the greatest trophy in the world. Their latest World Cup victory was particularly special: It was the first World Cup win after the reunification of Germany. (Previous Cups were won as West Germany.) This team, on and off the pitch, believes in working together and building for the future. Will that experience give them the confidence to win back-to-back Cups?

KOREA REPUBLIC

COACH: SHIN TAE-YONG
TEAM NICKNAME: TAEGEUK WARRIORS
PREVIOUS APPEARANCES: 9 • **WINS:** 0 • **FIFA RANKING:** 59

South Korea is historically one of the strongest teams in Asia. They've won more tournaments than any Asian country, including the AFC Asian Cup and the Asia Games. They've also participated in nine World Cups, even more than their main rival, fellow 2018 World Cup team Japan.

In the past, they've relied on the skills of Korean heroes like Cha Bum-kun, the nation's all-time leading goal scorer, and world-famous Park Ji-sung, the Manchester United fan favorite known as "Three-Lungs Park" because of his pace, relent-less determination, and outstanding endurance.

At this World Cup, South Korea does not have world-renowned names to rely on. Son Heung-min, the current squad's leading goal scorer, who plays for London club Tottenham Hotspur, and captain Ki Sung-yueng, who plays for Swansea City, will need to perform their all-out best if they want to make it past some incredibly tough opponents. Midfielders Koo Ja-cheol and Lee Chung-yong, along with veteran forward Lee Keun-ho, will join them in the attack.

MEXICO

COACH: JUAN CARLOS OSORIO
TEAM NICKNAME: EL TRI ("THE THREE COLOR")
PREVIOUS APPEARANCES: 15 • WINS: 0 • FIFA RANKING: 16

Mexico is no stranger to the World Cup—it has reached the knockout rounds of every tournament since 1994. El Tri boasts veterans like goalkeeper Guillermo Ochoa, defenders Héctor Moreno and Miguel Layún, and exciting goal scorers Andrés Guardado, the captain, and charismatic forward Javier "Chicharito" Hernández.

Chicharito ("Little Pea") is Mexico's all-time leading goal scorer. At club level Chicharito is sometimes known as a "super sub"—a player who can come off the bench to dramatically impact games. But for his country, Chicharito is a central figure. Small, fast, and sneaky, he'll be constantly slipping past defenders and trying to poach goals. Mexico's

veteran players are joined by exciting young talent like 22-year-old Hirving "Chucky" Lozano. This will be Lozano's first World Cup, but he's already scored game winners for his country.

But Mexico isn't without vulnerabilities. Much to the distress of Mexican fans, Coach Juan Carlos Osorio has loved tinkering with lineups and formations. If players don't have a consistent system in which to play, will they know their roles well enough come game day? Unfortunately for fans everywhere, Mexico has also suffered defensive injuries in the past month. This could rob key players—and spectators—of the chance to see a full-strength squad in action.

SWEDEN

COACH: JANNE ANDERSSON
PREVIOUS APPEARANCES: 11 • WINS: 0 • FIFA RANKING: 18

Despite the never-ending rumors of a dramatic return, this squad will be playing at the 2018 World Cup without Zlatan Ibrahimovic, the iconic Swedish hero and soccer world phenomenon who retired from the national team in 2016. (Although with a player as recognized, charismatic, and full of surprises as Ibrahimovic, expect his shadow to loom large at Swedish games.)

Even without its superstar forward, Sweden earns its high world ranking with hard work and solid performances in every area of the pitch. Veteran Andreas Granqvist, the Swedish captain, runs a close-knit, well-disciplined defense with 23-year-old Victor Lindelöf. A hero both on and off the pitch, Granqvist has impressed his teammates with excellent tackling and delighted them with friendly locker-room shenanigans. (He let Lindelöf and forward John Guidetti shave his head to celebrate Sweden's World Cup qualification!)

In the midfield, Emil Forsberg could be a standout player for Sweden. His efforts on the left wing have helped him score six goals. Meanwhile, up top, striker Marcus Berg will try to fill the immense hole left behind by Ibrahimovic.

GROUP G

BELGIUM • ENGLAND • PANAMA • TUNISIA

JUNE 18
Belgium vs. Panama
Tunisia vs. England

JUNE 23
Belgium vs. Tunisia

JUNE 24
England vs. Panama

JUNE 28
England vs. Belgium
Panama vs. Tunisia

Group G has no clear favorite, but it pits star-studded Belgium and England against gutsy underdogs Panama and Tunisia. Will the European teams live up to big expectations from their home fans? Or will Panama and Tunisia surprise the world?

BELGIUM

COACH: ROBERTO MARTÍNEZ
TEAM NICKNAME: THE RED DEVILS
PREVIOUS APPEARANCES: 12 • WINS: 0 • FIFA RANKING: 5

Belgium's roster may well be made up of the "golden generation"—a squad in which the lucky nation's most talented players are all reaching their peak at the same time. Forwards like Romelu Lukaku, Dries Mertens, and Eden Hazard almost never fail to offer dynamic play, so look for them to create some of the most exciting goals of the tournament. They'll be helped in the midfield by the likes of Kevin De Bruyne, Manchester City's sensational playmaker. This wily soccer wonder has a knack for slipping the ball past tough defenses and awing spectators with dazzling technical skill.

Belgium coach Roberto Martínez has encouraged his side to throw everything they have into their attack—but this will also leave Belgium extremely vulnerable if they're not careful. Vincent Kompany will try to keep things under control in the heart of Belgium's defense, but with so many other players constantly engaged in forward play, they're liable to concede plenty of chances—and goals. Belgium's fun, risky setup promises a party up front and potential chaos at the back; if you're looking for a team to surprise you (for better or worse!), look no further.

ENGLAND

COACH: GARETH SOUTHGATE
TEAM NICKNAME: THE THREE LIONS
PREVIOUS APPEARANCES: 14 • **WINS:** 0 • **FIFA RANKING:** 15

Over the past few European and world tournaments, England has developed an unfortunate reputation for excellent qualifying results followed by soul-crushing early exits. But the guard has changed at the Three Lions. Leaders from past tournaments—Steven Gerrard, Frank Lampard, and Wayne Rooney—have retired, and a bright, determined lineup of new talent has emerged. UK soccer fans will recognize many of the players from the Premier League's top clubs, including Manchester United, Chelsea, Arsenal, Manchester City, Liverpool, and Tottenham Hotspur.

Every area of the pitch is a strength and a weakness for England. Defenders John Stones and Kyle Walker are talented but inconsistent. Eric Dier and Jordan Henderson brilliantly help to protect the defense from midfield, but those defensive instincts often slow down play. On their day, goal scorers like Jesse Lingard, Jamie Vardy, Dele Alli, Harry Kane, Raheem Sterling, and young Marcus Rashford can terrify a defense—but they sometimes struggle to break down stubborn teams.

The England squad has worked well together through qualifying and look ready to battle their way out of their group. Will this finally be the tournament where England lives up to expectations?

PANAMA

COACH: HERNÁN DARÍO GÓMEZ
TEAM NICKNAME: LOS CANALEROS
PREVIOUS APPEARANCES: 0 • WINS: 0 • FIFA RANKING: 56

Fans of the US Men's National Team will be all too familiar with Panama. They edged their way into the World Cup ahead of the Yanks late last year. This will be the small Central American nation's first-ever World Cup appearance—upon hearing the news of the team's historic achievement, the president of Panama wasted no time declaring a national holiday!

Since qualification, though, the team has had a tough time preparing for the tournament. Their dramatic late-game win against Costa Rica was followed by losses in friendly matches to Denmark and Switzerland. As newcomers to the Cup, they'll need to settle on a style of play and team setup to stand a chance against the more experienced opposition.

Their coach, Hernán Darío Gómez, is exactly what they need. He's helped three different teams—Colombia, Ecuador, and now Panama—to the World Cup. With Panama, he's built a squad around tough defender Román Torres and forward threats Gabriel Torres and Blas Pérez. With an experienced coach and a few disciplined veterans, can Panama get its first World Cup win?

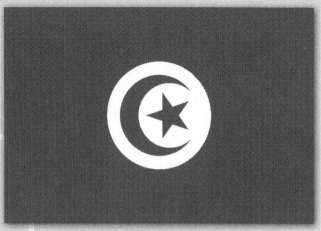

TUNISIA

COACH: NABIL MAÂLOUL
TEAM NICKNAME: THE EAGLES OF CARTHAGE
PREVIOUS APPEARANCES: 4 • WINS: 0 • FIFA RANKING: 27

Tunisia is ready to make a dramatic World Cup comeback after missing out on the past three tournaments. They've never made it past the group stages, and since they'll be facing tough group opposition in this Cup, they'll need to up their game like never before.

They should feel excited for the challenge—Tunisia went undefeated in qualification and has a squad full of little-known but nevertheless dangerous talent. Aymen Abdennour, Tunisia's key defender, will need to use his experience playing club soccer in Europe to organize and lead their back line. Further, forwards Wahbi Khazri and Youssef Msakni must work together to find goals for the Eagles of Carthage.

Tunisia is also more flexible than other teams in the tournament. Their coach has successfully helped them practice a few different playing formations, so they can seamlessly adapt to various opponents; if they need to get goals, they can throw more men forward, and they can just as readily hunker down if they need to play more defensively. Will this advantage help them overcome the challenges of Group G?

GROUP H

COLOMBIA • JAPAN • POLAND • SENEGAL

JUNE 19
Colombia vs. Japan
Poland vs. Senegal

JUNE 24
Japan vs. Senegal
Poland vs. Colombia

JUNE 28
Japan vs. Poland
Senegal vs. Colombia

Group H doesn't have any of the tournament favorites—and that's why it might be the toughest and most exciting group of the Cup! Colombia, Japan, Poland, and Senegal are relatively evenly matched, so anything could happen.

COLOMBIA

COACH: JOSÉ PÉKERMAN
TEAM NICKNAME: LOS CAFETEROS
PREVIOUS APPEARANCES: 5 • WINS: 0 • FIFA RANKING: 13

Colombia lost its 2014 World Cup quarterfinal game to Brazil, but not before winning the hearts of spectators around the world. The players' iconic salsa-dance goal celebration became one of the highlights of the last Cup, so fans will be hoping for plenty of goals this time around.

In 2014, Colombia's young #10, James Rodríguez, rose to the occasion after the devastating injury of forward Radamel "El Tigre" Falcao. After scoring six goals, Rodríguez won the Golden Boot, awarded to the Cup's highest goal scorer, and became a hero to his country. Since then, he's been playing for some of the biggest teams in Europe and gaining invaluable experience at the international level.

This year, Rodríguez's right-hand man, Juan Cuadrado, is recovering from injury and may not make the tournament. But Falcao is back and ready to captain Colombia through another outstanding World Cup. In 2017, El Tigre became the country's all-time top goal scorer. Could Falcao or Rodríguez bring another surprise Golden Boot back to Colombia?

JAPAN

COACH: AKIRA NISHINO
TEAM NICKNAME: THE SAMURAI BLUES
PREVIOUS APPEARANCES: 5 • WINS: 0 • FIFA RANKING: 55

Japan is one of the strongest teams in Asia, with a long history but a new coach. Akira Nishino joined the Samurai Blues just months before the tournament; they had already qualified for the World Cup, but found themselves struggling to find wins. Many coaches would be intimidated by such a big, sudden responsibility. But Nishino has remained fearless, and wants the same from his players. He's promised to bring fans attack-focused soccer and disciplined, skilled performances. Nishino—a former Japanese national team player himself—has the respect of the team.

Like their rivals, South Korea, Japan doesn't have a world-famous player to base the squad around; what they lack in star power, they must build together as a unit. A few key players, like midfielder Shinji Kagawa and defenders Maya Yoshida and Hiroki Sakai, could give Japan stability in defense and creative options going forward. But Japan faces another huge challenge: All three players will be recovering from injury, so playing time might have to be limited. It may be up to emerging talent like forward Takuma Asano to find goals and wins.

In past tournaments, Japan has made it out of the group stages twice but never passed the round of 16. Does the new coach have what it takes to guide this team to and through the knockout rounds?

POLAND

COACH: ADAM NAWAŁKA

PREVIOUS APPEARANCES: 7 • WINS: 0 • FIFA RANKING: 7

Polish captain Robert Lewandowski could likely be a star at this tournament. He's one of the best forwards around—an excellent dribbler, a sneaky poacher of goals, and a strong striker with a knack for hitting powerful headers into the net. Lewandowski is already Poland's all-time leading scorer. He scored 16 goals in qualifying for this World Cup, more than any other player in qualifying, and he's a favorite to win this year's Golden Boot (awarded to the player who scores the most goals at the Cup). If Poland moves on from Group H, he might also find himself playing Germany and friends from his German club team,

Bayern Munich—but Poland has to win group games first.

Lewandowski isn't the only one to watch for Poland. Striker Arkadiusz Milik has less experience than his older captain, but he also has a great instinct for finding the back of the net. Winger Kamil Grosicki helped create chances for Poland at Euro 2016, and if he can do it again, Poland will have multiple threats going forward. Poland gave up a lot of goals in qualifying, so look for goalkeepers Łukasz Fabiański and Wojciech Szczęsny to be more disciplined with their defenders at the tournament.

SENEGAL

COACH: ALIOU CISSÉ
NICKNAME: LES LIONS DE LA TERANGA ("THE LIONS OF TERANGA")
PREVIOUS APPEARANCES: 1 • WINS: 0 • FIFA RANKING: 23

Senegal's team brings together the past and future in famous coach Aliou Cissé and sensational player Sadio Mané. Cissé, who retired from the Senegal squad, played as a midfielder and defender throughout Europe during his club career. One of his greatest triumphs as a player was his outstanding performance for Senegal in the 2002 World Cup. Now Cissé hopes to let a new generation make its mark: "That team already created its bit of history, and now it's up to this one to create its own."

Enter Mané, the lightning-fast winger known for terrorizing defenses down his side of the pitch. His quick turns, explosive pace, impressive dribbling, and clinical finishing have been crucial to the success of his club team, Liverpool. He's the Senegalese linchpin, but far from the only exciting name on the team's roster. Mané is joined by Kalidou Koulibaly in defense, Idrissa Gueye in midfield, and exciting young forward Keita Baldé, who turned 23 just a few months before the tournament.

This hardworking team knows how to play together, play for one another, and have fun on the pitch; when they score, keep watch for some of Mané's fun dance celebrations.

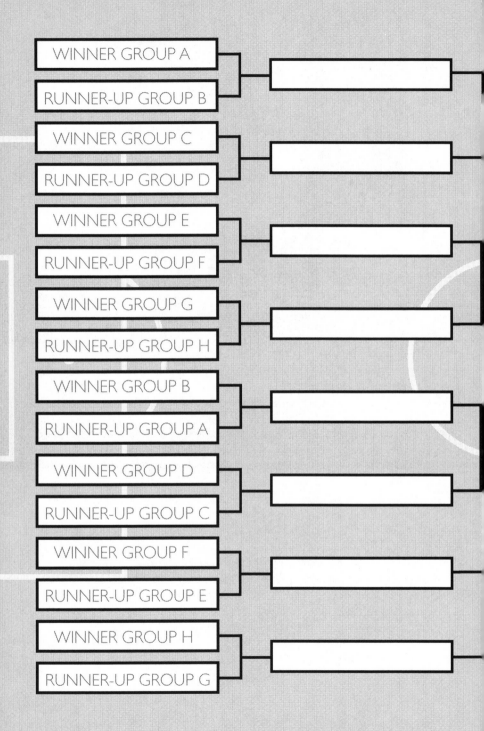

KNOCKOUT ROUND BRACKET

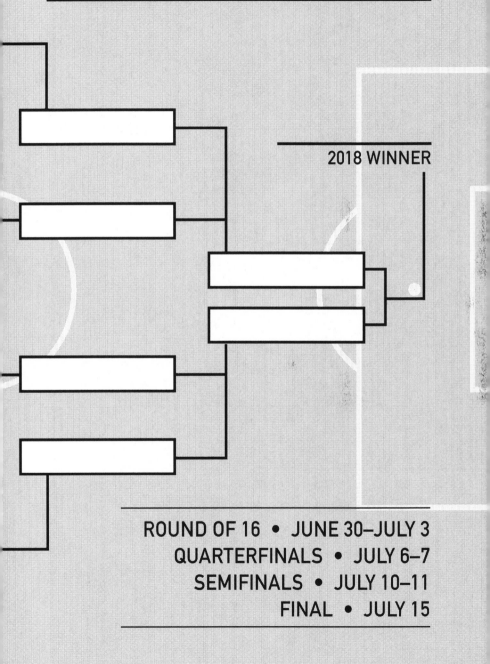

2018 WINNER

ROUND OF 16 • JUNE 30–JULY 3
QUARTERFINALS • JULY 6–7
SEMIFINALS • JULY 10–11
FINAL • JULY 15

MEXICO

PANAMA

COSTA RICA

COLOMBIA

PERU

BRAZIL

URUGUAY

ARGENTINA

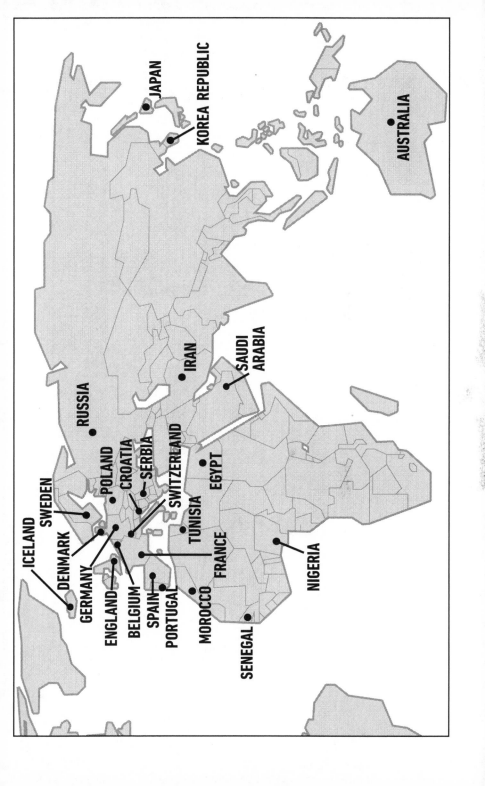

PAST WINNERS

1930	URUGUAY
1934	ITALY
1938	ITALY
1950	URUGUAY
1954	WEST GERMANY
1958	BRAZIL
1962	BRAZIL
1966	ENGLAND
1970	BRAZIL
1974	WEST GERMANY
1978	ARGENTINA
1982	ITALY
1986	ARGENTINA
1990	WEST GERMANY
1994	BRAZIL
1998	FRANCE
2002	BRAZIL
2006	ITALY
2010	SPAIN
2014	GERMANY

Made in the USA
San Bernardino, CA
18 June 2018